Penguins

This book belongs to

_____

Written by Tapasi De
Illustrated by Suman S. Roy

Penguins are aquatic, flightless birds. They are found mostly in Antarctica.

Penguins are stocky, short-legged birds.

Their bodies are black on the back and white in front.

This is called 'counter-shading'. It is a form of hiding that helps the penguins to remain safe in water.

Penguins do have wing-bones. But they are flipper-like which help them in swimming.

Penguins, who live closer to the Equator eat fish and penguins closer to Antarctica eat squids and krills.

Larger penguin are found in colder climates whereas smaller penguins live in warmer climate.

The Macaroni Penguins are the highest in terms of their numbers.

Penguins have no fear of humans. They come to meet travellers without hesitation.

Penguins can spend most of their lives in water. They also hunt in water.

Penguins catch their food in their beaks and swallow them whole.

The Emperor Penguin lives in the coldest environment on Earth.

The Emperor Penguin is the largest penguin.

Penguins are social birds. They form large groups or 'rookeries' that include thousands of penguins!

On land, penguins use their tails and wings to balance themselves.

Penguins have an average sense of hearing.

When penguins dive, they reach up to a speed of 6 to 12 kilometer per hour.

Small penguins do not dive deep. They catch their prey near the surface of water. Their dives last only for one or two minutes.

Larger penguins can dive deep when needed. They dive upto 2,000 feet and it may last for up to 22 minutes!

Penguins also jump with both feet together to move quickly or to cross steep surfaces.

Penguins waddle on their feet or slide on their bellies on the snow.

Penguins can see clearly underwater.

Penguins have a thick layer of feathers that keeps them warm.

Male penguins often huddle together to keep warm. They also rotate their positions to give each penguin a turn to be in the centre of the pack.

Penguins can drink salty water. They throw out salt through their nose.

Penguin eggs are smaller than any other bird species.

A penguin baby is called a 'hatching'.

If a penguin mother loses its baby, it sometimes tries to steal another mother's chick.

New words to learn

acquatic	swallow
flightless	rookeries
tropical	prey
stocky	rocky
Antarctica	enemies
counter-shading	rotate
flipper	hatching
krills	chick
climate	
species	
beaks